As to Myself

VOL. 2

As to Myself

VOL. 2

DAVID WRIGHT

DIPS
Publishing

As to Myself, Volume 2
Copyright ©2017 by David Wright
All rights reserved.

Published by DIP'S Publishing
Cleveland, Ohio
www.thinkforyourself.life

ISBN:978-1-946818-05-8
Printed in the United States of America

I dedicate this book to my Grandma Smith. I dedicate this book to her because of all the time we shared; over the summers of my life. As a trestle, you were the sternest and the straightest. Grandma you were firm, but I did get and receive love from you. The love you offered was just different. If given the choice back then, I would have refused it. But I'm so thankful that back then, kids weren't allowed to choose. You were indeed scary, but under your rough exterior was a grandmother. A no non-sense, no holds barred; Grandmother. If we got out of line, we were dealt with. But under the lion's paw, the cubs did play. I thank you Grandma for all you taught. Being from Mississippi, I know that in your day; you saw much. I know that your anger and bitter ways had to come from somewhere. I just know how you were with us, thank you. You taught me how to save and a lot about being a man. Rest in peace, Effie Smith. If anybody does, you deserve it.

CONTENTS

As to Myself

VOL. 2

Father God

Hear my prayer, let it not go unanswered but be heard right now and addressed even more swiftly! We are your chosen, led from one place into another but never moving! Lost as if we journeyed by ship halfway around the globe and were dispersed to scatter like lava out of a volcano. From living in the spirit to living through the flesh, a journey from heaven to hell made overnight. Usually journeyed so quickly that footprints are light so no tracks are left making backtracking impossible. Many walk the sands of time and life lost as a soul with no body, looking everywhere but within for the truth and passage to return home! Father God wash away our amnesia so that we may remember the way...back, to you! Let us stop worshipping false Gods of Mercy, compassion and weakness. Let us gain your strength Father God, the strength you provided Sampson, King David and Jesus with to over come in their times of need! We too have enemies, Father God aid us in our hour of tribulation that we may once again praise, worship and follow! Let us come together under covenant, that no man shall break, compromise or disrespect. Father God we Pray that you hear and answer, not now but right now. Sincerely the children of Jacob!

My allegiance

Is pledged to you, wherever you lead I will follow! You have given me so much, your blessings truly are pouring down, shaken, packed and still overflowing. I accept your will and your way; your slightest whisper of a command do I hear and follow! The pages you left, I read and they indeed nourish my soul! My faith grows as my bounty does also, hand in hand so I prosper and learn! Giving and getting as I journey! My body has been truly blessed with a mind to want! To want to know, to want to learn, to want to share! I pledge my allegiance to you oh Lord, you promised never to leave nor forsake me! And I promise that I will never turn my back to you because, I know that your my Father! Let this covenant called My Allegiance last for eternity!

The Baptismal

Can It honestly change me?, I can go in dirty and come out cleansed? A bath made in heaven for my body? One to be made clean, to be forgiven and to start anew, for that is my question posed! Or is this a spiritual transformation at hand? Are the waters that clean me, my thoughts becoming controlled? For I am that I am! So that I think I receive; and if controlled, trained, harnessed and utilized, my thoughts could bring me blessings? Me meaning all, because what am I? If not apart. Yes I must be made clean to join, less my dirty ways corrupt the whole. Where is my place in this pure thought oasis, my baptismal is your invitation; Lord! I long to play my part, even though my role is carried out by destiny. Change my way of thinking that I may acknowledge you fully. Being made more able with every dip in you cleansing training. Stronger and stronger, now able to guide my mind. Clean—The Baptismal.

Inside my mind

In my mind I am guarded, intrigued and made to feel safe. I have practiced thinking, so my mind is now my sanctuary. It is inside my mind that I dwell and claim freedom but it is only outside my mind where I can serve others physically and his will be done. It is inside my mind that I come up with the greatest good for all but only outside my mind that I can execute, express and let that good facilitate greatness! It is said that the Lord works in mysterious ways; only because the pickings are slim of those that will do his biddings of love. If we all had love inside our minds, it would be in our hands and he could mold this plastic and work wonders through us, that would be common because we all could mesmerize with our faith. In my mind I must keep balance however so I do not blur and cross the boundaries of sanity! Therefore the greater my external service the more comfortable inside will I be. Able to make room for new thoughts! and continue to serve!

In the shade

In the shade without a fear or a care, left alone to feel and believe. To listen to the words spoken by the wind as it rustles so softly through the leaves. To interpret the language the blue jay speaks. As he lands looking pretty then goes. The squirrels climb up and down the trees chasing closely one another in tow. As I loose myself in the world inside the world that I live each day. Usually overlooking these things Just makes me think what would life be like if they went away. If the shade was gone no butterflies flew and the grass was beige not green. What would life be like if the sun didn't come up and the birds had no songs to sing. Would we notice or over look as we do now the wonders that the father has set I'm sure we'de complain for we notice the mundane. But not all the beauty we get I refuse to take for granted another sunrise or perfect day that's he's made. And when the sun seems to get too hot, well I just admire what he's given in the shade.

Can't you tell

Can't you tell how blessed I am? The spirit that is in me is in me! Realized and known. Communicated with, daily. One I am with the three! Can't you tell? I am different than I used to be! Not perfect but making the journey. And no journey is complete without a destination!

*P*atience

I strive for perfection but have not yet achieved. Wrong I will be in my search, I will require patience from life to grow. As I require so much why do I offer so little. I feel no empathy, only my agenda. So I push often times over and through others. Because I am striving that makes it ok. I am no better than those who oppress me when I oppress others. We all use, it is the misuse that raises concern. I must be fair! I must be Patient enough to listen, patient enough to be concerned with something other than myself. Patient enough to stop and give of myself that which I require most! Whatever it may be. To feel the spirit of absolute control, that breeds patience. It breeds understanding; enough to know that by the grace of God I go! In the light, in the darkness in the deep. But it is by grace I go, and by his patience I am allowed to journey and explore. Let us give to have and study to know patience.

I truly AM

Every name you can think of to describe perfect, for in his image I am made! As we all are, powerful and perfect in every regard. Able to understand and know! I truly am as we all are, only as blessed, special, and stupendous as I give myself credit for being. That's why I am, everything, under the sun and more, for I truly am my fathers son! But the power lies in the fact that I know that I TRULY AM!

Acres and Acres

So much space, so much material to use! I can build anything. Acres and Acres of fertile ground! Whatever I plant will produce that unto it's kind! I see apartment buildings as far as the eye can see. I see a man that cares about and does his best to understand others. I see perfect health, I see long life with a sound mind. I see family and loved ones always around, I see prosperity for friends and wealth for all those associated! As thoughts are things, what I see are my seeds. I plant in faith, with no doubt so I do not check on progress, I only await the harvest. Watering with my desire and feelings, while shining the sun of my WILL! As I sew the greatest possible thoughts, I reap in kind it's physical equivalent! As the farmer plants corn and gets fields of corn. I plant my seeds of thought and receive acres of the same as well. As far as the eye can see, I can plant a crop. Some plant in square feet while others utilize the acres and acres of their minds!

Along the way

Along the way I have experienced every pain I have ever caused. Life is funny that way, it lets you think you've escaped. Only to repay that which you owe at the most unexpected time.

Along the way I have lost many a friend, some from natural causes; some from lack of understanding. It's strange that in apparent loss, you gain the most. That when things are at their worst, you receive the greatest insight. Along the way I have wanted to give up many a time. That I didn't I guess is why I love me so! Everyone's along the way will be different, notice the scenery as you travel. Who knows if you will pass by that way again. Along the way may be rough, just make it! Make it if only to encourage another to journey! Be sincere as you can in that your character is the road you will travel. Until I die I will explore, I will roam, I will journey. I hope to see you, along the way!

Come in out of the rain

Enough is enough. STOP. We are out of control! We must come in out the rain to get dry and rethink the position we have chosen.

My youth, I love you because your my future, you will carry on what I leave. Or it will be turned over to another. Come in out of the rain or catch pneumonia and die. That simple it is but when one is not brought up in the beauty of simplicity. A simple thing is not so beautiful but common. If but one comes in and grabs a towel to dry off, I have achieved much-others will follow. Understand with your whole body that jail is not for you! How special and creative you are, even if you have never been told. What laces your insides, is a very small piece of what it takes to make the sun rise each day. Come in, dry off and get smart so you can meet the challenges of good weather and not constantly be ducking that which seeks to take your health. You are young and strong but you must gain that mental strength that can only be learned in a dry environment. Come in and begin to get better!

TFOAGM

Ahh what wonders lie ahead, what power do we posses.

In the mind, imagination and the love in mans faithful breast.

If with the faith of a mustard seed A mountain he can move.

With the faith of a full-grown man what wonders could he prove.

Cures to all ails, diseases even more!

Could he feed the multitudes upon the oceans floor?

Could he get man to introspect and dig deep into his design.

To find the piece of the grand architect we all emulate in mind.

We are all but one degree removed from that we love the most.

So who dares here—to draw that near

And realize what we should already know.

That kings and queens may conquer things But that does not really last.

It's the faith that man musters when he can that will survive times pass.

With the faith of a mustard seed

It's said mountains he can move.

So with the faith of a full grown man—who knows what else is true?

Looking up

Do I pray, do I stare or do I just contemplate your splendor? How you separated the waters to create heaven and earth. Or how with mathematical precision everything moves. Never off, never out of sequence, he may not come when you need him but he's always on time. I look up in wonder and aww always because your shockingly amazing, never to disappoint! From the rainbow that reminds us of your covenant with the earth; never to destroy it again. To every desire put in the hearts of man to be extracted! Looking up, I bow my head in honor and respect to my leader, my king, my Lord, my Law! I journey with you unflinchingly, the more faith I will have when our road is darkest. I will lean looking up and put my trust in you.

The Source

I AM, able to see and feel all that I can fathom! I think along the lines of understanding, I want my thought to transform itself-to align with the greatness of you! I will mold my piece of " THE PLASTIC" into your shape and form! Un plagued by the poisons of flesh and the restraints of fear, the devils biggest tool! I want to resemble he that is in me, so much so that my earthly form is no longer recognizable. All you will see is the Source when you see me! The source of everything worth anything! That one we see in prayer! I want to grow my fledgling bit of faith into a full grown Phoenix! Able to conquer by faith! Walking by it alone and not by sight, using more than the ten percent I'm accustomed to but learning how to work and utilize the whole 100 percent of your bounty! Life is the school of you, the university of the SOURCE!

More years more days more hours more minutes

Time—as it passes I grow, so blessed I am to be a part of God's plan. My role not known at times intricately still I play a part. Amazing at the same time expected sincerely embodying creation. My mother spoke of glory finally I see for myself. My years spent in church playing hide and go seek must have paid off. My mother would be amazed the scriptures I retained. Time is passing as we speak. I grow better with my every breath. The same substance that was amidst the first thought electric stimulation Exist in me time moves vibrates inside even my very blood. I feel favored exalted destined for better greater ground to explore The need for need is not needed. I see only faith as I journey unshakable. Unfadeable, excellent, perfect in every way. Able to stand the test of time.

Your lows will be fewer

When you stop doubting and believe! Believe in yourself, in this process called nature, in your creator called God! Have faith in you like one does about tomorrow coming. You have more control over your mind than you do over the dawn of a new day. Your thoughts are why your tomorrows play out as they do. Your lows will be fewer when you understand how all are favored, how we are so pampered as to have gotten what we aspire to. All we want upon demand and command! As we desire what's undesirable we complain to our God who says your lows would be fewer if you would change your mind. Change those thoughts and let them be studied upon before had so that your outcome satisfies instead of torments.

Rock bottom

Looking up from on top it's lonely when you make it alone. I let competition dictate my thoughts now friends are scarce; misery is my only company. I gained the world but daily look for my soul; it eludes me like a shadow taunting me but never close enough to hold on to. I thought I knew what I was giving up. I freely return everything just for one to call friend. Not to die alone if only to take time to talk or hear or just appear. I will make it worth your while never answered. I have grown so distant not even my prayers are heard my thoughts are to heavy to travel. Too filled with the wait of pity shame and what's to come. Where will I end possessions are a cold friend. Only here to amuse himself and leave me as soon as I spend you. Woe is me I have made a mistake, chosen finance over faith and success over love. At rock bottom I sit rightly served—cold and alone.

My voice/why me

Where did it come from?, I recognize we are joined, but why have you chosen me to speak through. I could have been a dog or dinosaur, or just one without the want to know. I ask again, why me? You have blessed me with an ear to hear but also a voice to describe my thoughts. Coupled with that I am busting with a spirit of understanding. My voice, why me I say again? You are so mighty you can do anything through the millions you create, daily. Why me?, the specialness of my voice is so appreciated. I will use it to serve you, with my every breath and thought. It's not out of disrespect I ask why me but out of love and admiration. I ask because you could have chosen so many. But you picked me, to give a voice.

What you don't know about me

That I did not know I resembled God, but now I do! I used to think that I had to accept what was given, because who am I to question! But now I know that my dominion over this domain is apparent in my thoughts then my character followed by my actions.

What you don't know about me is that I did not always understand that my thoughts order my steps! Nor was I willing to accept my part in beauty or the destruction of such with the smallest amount of ill will regarded. I am told to extend my very best, not for the sake of the receiver but for that of the one who gives! You are only being generous to yourself and your own situation. What you do not know about me is that it is my pleasure to facilitate the truth, if it should mean my life. If I should die before I wake, I pray my soul the Law should take. What you don't know about me is I know God is inside of me and I release him with great joy!

Complete

All the way rounded out! Able to understand is what is meant. Connecting with others and able to realize what you are worth! Priceless we are!, but if you have $1 million and never spend it and die did you ever really have it? Power not used is power lost, and how truly powerful we are. Or are you? Are you complete? Do you seek that end with your existence?, completeness. On the road to such is as good as being but nothing in nature sits still. It is either living or dying, complete or incomplete! We are all perfect, but you must realize this image of his you were made in to attain perfection.

Courage

Not many can make this journey, let me rephrase that. Not many are successful at running this race and crossing the finish line in tact. One told me it was hard out here for pimp I told him change professions cuz it's easy out here for a child of God! I plan courageously and execute fearlessly, without a care in the world because all things work for the greater good for those that believe! My power is in my courage my courage is just another word for faith, I fear no man. And I love my father with all my thoughts! With my father being creator of the universe, whom shall I fear. Fear is but the absence of courage! So with courage one can have no fear, simple it is but complexly explained. Study for yourself and clear up your understanding, have FAITH! HAVE COURAGE! IN YOU.

The rear view

Never will I feel this way again, FEAR you are a problem that I will now and forever be seeing in the distance! I have given you too much!, to much thought, too much concentration, too much of me!

My very ESSENCE, DESIRE and WILL not stolen, but given away, time and time again, continuously. As I embark on this new journey of love, of hope and of finding myself; Fear you seem to be getting smaller and smaller in my rear view!

Do I fit in?

I look so different do I fit in

Am I the same as you?

I have often wondered while I sat and
pondered under the skies of blue.

For if we are the same why do we fight, argue and hate.

We were made in his image from the very beginning let's join and do things that are great. Do I fit in? I dare say no. Because none of us really get along. For if I fit in, then you are my kin, and together we should stand strong. We are all one, endowed with a piece of the creator when life began. So am I now a fool because I ask...

...knowing that I do fit in?

When

I'm lonely I know it won't last; because with you I'm never alone!, when I'm happy, I take advantage of the feeling; I remember it in case I need it when I'm not! When I'm sad, I think about the things in my life then I go back to the thought that made it; and get rid of it! When I am great full, I praise; I let my God know for what and why I love him so. I let him know that I could do nothing without his power that I am lost without the spirit. When I'm scared of the outcome, of whatever I summon my strength! The strength of everything I have ever made it through, my testimony is my road map to success. It lets me know I can't lose, because I've won in the face of defeat so many times before. When I love, I love hard because I don't know if this is my last time with this opportunity. I want love to be last on my lips and first on my mind! When I am here, I want to make an impact so when I am gone, you remember me!

My interpretation of life

As your thoughts dictate your life our views on this subject may be different. I feel only love even when hate is thrust upon me. I know men understand not that which they do. I can only have forgiveness in my heart if that is what I want to receive when I fall short. How can I for a minute say that my days given to me by thee are not exquisite. Any complaint is an attempt for pity and with me being born so perfect how could I Jockey for such. Even one who was been born handicapped is perfectly suited for what life has called him for. We are all created in the image of the almighty there never is one greater or weaker than another. We have all been indowed with the same power of spirit! I praise your name for all that comes my way, continue to mold and shape me oh grand architect. As you are, leave me when your done!

Eventually

I'm going to make it all the way so blessed and highly favored that you will not be able to deny me. As the cosmos and all it has to offer unfolds and finds an exit through my form. Expression is my nature I am as flawless as birth! Able to understand the riddles of time by sheer intuition. Eventually you will see, Eventually it will come full circle as I rise, my mental only grows. Help is on the way. Eventually we will understand that God is in and not up, able to be talked to at will as he is omnipotent a piece of me is always with him as he is Omni present a piece of him is always with me. Eventually we will teach our children to understand that greater is he that is in me than thee that is within the world, mathematics is very important but an understanding of the piece of God you share with all of creation is of far greater consequence. Eventually is on its way!

What if

What if I understood, gave you my best always!

Imagine if collectively we felt love as a mob does hate.

So much is accomplished by hate in seconds ... what if love accomplished the infinite?!

What if we were too scared to loose and stayed away from our brothers only to suffer in silence?

To be alone in a crowded room what if I read your thoughts and held you when you needed it Or gave you directions to the way to your soul when you were lost What if we listened to each other to listen and not respond What if I respected myself then could love you Would this help the world, us, each other?

What if it did what would you do?

Would you do the what ifs or nothing?

What if this was the way to do unto others The rule of gold we learned in what seems like a distant memory A lifetime ago simple it is but difficult it's made from the vine we are if I cut your supply do I not loose my own what if I understood?

What brings you peace

What makes you feel the way that you feel when you feel at peace? Amazing it be if collectively we could bottle and give all a piece. Then that feeling we'd share—and all be repaired, fixed for the very last time. So in search of that truth, let's start this journey in earnest hopes that we find. The feeling you get originates from what is the question I pose to you all. For if we can pinpoint the feeling find it at will when in need all you'd need do is call. Perplexing for sure but not so much so when two or more are gathered in truth. Seems clear to me the feeling I seek is buried deep down in you. I say that because of the happiness brought whenever you I seem to find. But I feel the same when merely thinking your name, so is happiness all state of mind?

I'd like to say because if that's the way then now the ball will roll. What brings us peace is different to say the least. But now you know it's in your control.

Chapters

Who am I? Pages turn in my life I was once unsure but through pursuit, vision is becoming clearer. I change could not always feel as I do will one day not be able to feel as I do now. I change for evolution's sake I grow, parts of me die, I'm me. I was alone but changed into a family, caring for those that in a blink of an eye will soon care for me I've learned to take advantage of my thoughts and not to simply think for thinking's sake. There is power in my pages where the end is marked, what I have created will turn so that it is endless! Our story. Only I close the book! My I is the new that touches every I after this a piece of me to continue in different form. Fire never dies, only changes torches. But burns! My part in creation will continue. I exist. I am story. I am life. I AM.

What do you want of me

I ask because I truly am ready to answer the call. In the past with honesty put first I must admit that I lived a life regarding only myself. But not anymore, I ask what do you want of me because I am tired of serving me and now live to serve you! My accomplishments are hollow and done in vain when you are not the goal of attainment, what do you want of me. My years of self service have turned into decades but my days that have equaled to months in service of you has multiplied those months into what feels like a lifetime of committed service! What do you want of me, my next step will be my all time greatest because I desire your opinion your will to dictate it's out come from the onset! What do you want of me, that I follow, lead, learn and teach is already done. My next move is yours oh Lord, where you say step, I will put my feet!

What if

We really cared about each other, would that change anything? Things are created by thought, so if I inspire contempt, does that set a chain of events in motion?! But if I inspire love, how would the landscape change? If love is sunlight and water, since it's all we need! Would everything benefit? What if we tried love instead of hate, even when a good case for hate could be made? What if I loved you when you hated me?, hate would no longer exist, for retaliation is just that; you respond in kind. You get what you give, what if we changed. I love you, because I love me!, I see clearly because I know what I look like to me. What if I stopped hating myself, what if I forgave myself for my past transgressions. What if I started with a clean slate with me? I don't hate you because I don't know you. What if everything started with me? What if this means, IF WE COULD CHANGE I, WE WOULD CHANGE THE WORLD!

My God

Do I look externally up or down or do I find you in places unknown? Or is it inside me where you reside a king that sits atop his throne? The throne above this physical pile of blood, of bones and veins. Such a lofty position truly a place for a king, to sit atop and reign. No better a kingdom for one to command than this empire I received from birth. I'm looking to find my God my friend to tell which thing to do first. Do I find you up, do I find you down, or do I find you hidden in men? If the latter part of the statement is true that means I find you within. Where have you been my king my friend I have been looking but could not find. He whispered and laughed, I giggled and gasped, "You've felt me in you the whole time."

Forgiveness

Who's fault it was fades away inevitably with the passing of time. Hours turn into days, years become lost when I'm sorry would have made it all fine. When prides in play love tends to suffer. Because pride will never be wrong forgiveness is lost my angry feelings are too this has gone on for far too long. Fathers and sons put the anger aside every second you've lost is enough. Mistakes were made wether you left or stayed. Let us love even if it must be tough. Brother and brother brother and sister and then sister and sister again. Come back together mend the fences let us be kids like when we were ten. At heart if nothing else back when you could do me no wrong. How it's funny we both are here but between us forgiveness is gone.

I can't even remember what started this feud let us forgive and forget, or say these same words alone either one of us. On that day in front of the others casket we sit.

The bird

If briefly I could have wings and soar up to the heavens close enough to touch. Without a care in the world I'd leave troubles to the ground and just fly up, up and up. How free it must feel to know that at best. You can change where you are in a blink. Man has been given that power over looked as it is in his divine ability to think. I soar with my thoughts and you on your wings to reach heights and limits unbound. On winds of Ether we are destined to reach the places in our hearts deep down. The places they fly on their wings in the air are the place that we go in our minds. So some are free to soar the heavens and explore while others are in cages and binds.

When I'm Lonely

I take time to think about how that could never be! How I'm apart of creation and everything that exist has a piece of me in it. Me being lonely with this in mind is absurd! How could I be ignorant enough to deny my birth right, the fact that I'm eternally connected to the vine! That when everything on earth was made, it was made with me in mind! How would the sun, moon grass, clouds and stars make me feel? That was definitely contemplated before the final mold of this everything was cast! My personality permeates the cosmos! When I feel alienated, I'm honest with myself in that I alone am at the base of that feeling of lonely, of singular, of separate! For who could convince me my father has turned away other than myself? If a stranger tried the same he would be laughed out of existence! It is only myself that could convince me that I'm lonely! Rather I will convince myself that I am an invaluable piece to this machine called humanity, called together, called life. Lonely, impossible unless I choose to be!

The remedy

To all that ales you is to love yourself! If you can't, if you won't, and if you don't; how can anyone else even begin too. Treat yourself as a stranger, and love that person every time you see them. They need you,. They need you to stop judging, stop ignoring and start loving. Just love because after all you do love them do you not. Yes we have other mountains to climb, but our first Mount Everest to conquer is loving ourselves, loving yourself is like the first warm day after winter to start spring. You should be able to summon that feeling on command. And that will be your searchlight, your remedy; for whenever darkness comes you can shine your light, love yourself and be made whole, be made happy again. You deserve the best, won't you start giving it? It's not from another, but from yourself you should get the most LOVE!

It's going to be ok

Grandma used to say that everything would be ok, that it would all work out. Even if I felt that not to be true, somehow, her words made the difference! Today, we, everyone of we, need to be that light to another. Everything will be ok, share that to receive that. Once said to another it is embraced deep inside of you. So you again and again tattoo on your soul that everything is going to be ok with every time it is said to another.

Once you believe that, you live that and the rest will fall in place! If you want to change your life, your circumstances change what you think. It doesn't have to be the truth right now, just say it. Believe in things that are not as tho they were. Grandma said it remember and we knew it wasn't true at the time but it helped. And that's why SHE SAID IT! EVERYTHING WILL BE OK! Wasn't it always for GRANDMA?

Each one teach one

Am I my brothers keeper?, is it up to me to teach him? Is it up to me to instruct those who don't know? The only way that this responsibility should be taken on is if I ever want to be helped! Or if I ever want to be told, when I don't know. We keep our brothers so that our brothers will keep us! No man is an island, we all will need. But that is the question, need what! We will need help, assistance, a kind word or just love! Let us extend ourselves to others so others will extend to us. And then being in need will never be! Each one teach one, as we give, we get!

Like a child

I attempt to understand what is my place to be understood! Knowledge is sometimes placed out of our reach purposely and like a child I climb the un steady book shelf intrigued by the shiny object. Any seeker of the truth will shed that knowledge is the ball that sometimes may get away from the child; that he chased in the street. Eager we are to better ourselves, babes we are when first starting. So chances do we take like a child, how we must give pleasure to God to watch his children grow and learn as he protects us from harm. At whatever age, he will never leave or forsake. Only guide, and like children sometimes we take instruction and sometimes we don't! As children we must remain humble and obedient until we learn, learn enough to know that this is a lifetime study. Yes we grow but will always be like children to he that created we! Let us pursue the land of milk and honey with child like vigor, and be fearless in thought less we miss our reward!

Clean

Made anew! The very second I received you, was I made whole! You being the truth of course, the way; the light! The moment I understood I myself barely could recognize me! Totally different, changed; now able to understand what before I couldn't. I know I am that I am, I have submerged myself into the abyss into the deep where you reside and come back better, come back brighter come back clean! This is not an effort of terror at the unclean, because we know clean just means an open mind. A mind able to discern, able to understand for themselves! Able to hear the word and accept it, we are made free by the waters of truth! Let us all submerge ourselves and become CLEAN!

We are like the leaves

In that we number in the billions here on earth at the same time. Some coming others going, some at the bottom, others at the top. Some to fall and get bagged never to be seen again! All meant to wither and die! Our lives come and go, like the days and seasons; with perfect timing. In nature we are brothers so why do we not connect. I have never seen a leaf worry, or fear the unknown, but we do. I have never seen a leaf step on another to rise, or mistreat for gain but we do. I have never seen a leaf feel like they didn't deserve life, abundance and the fullness there of, but we do. Let us pay attention to our brothers, God provides for them will he not do the same for us? For we are like the leaves! Deserving at all stages of life!

On the other hand

What if the teachings are wrong, what if all that is outside of us is all that matters! If the outside is the master of the in! If what we went through in a day dictated how we felt, if the things we saw were at the root of our desires! On the other hand if this was so, what a cage we would live in. Controlled like mice and studied in our habitats, the world being our cages. If that was the case how could one call on God, wouldn't that one be master trainer? For it takes no intelligence to design a prison! On the other hand what if accuracy lies in the FACT that all is within, that we are the masters of our movements in connection with thought and concentration! On this hand or any other, we summon our demons or Angels by the type of thoughts we entertain! We serve a GOD that has created his children as he is, sharing in an image that created the cosmos and spans eons of eternities! All basic, nothing complicated; it is only a truth that waits to be believed in!

Birthdays

Happy Birthday! But does this day find you happy? Or does it find you in fear? Fear of getting old, fear of dying, fear of failing again? How can you celebrate if your not proud of your progress? If you haven't gotten as far as you'd like to be and time is closing how do you embrace that? You don't! Life is for the living and your goals are for the attaining! But you can't attain what you don't set! How can you believe and dream big if you don't first cultivate your faith, it only takes a mustard seed worth to be great! It is never too late to create what you desire, as the sun shines so do you create- if that is your will. For it must be done! On earth as it is in heaven! So what do you dream, if you don't dream no disappointment can you hold. But if you dream without fear, you will have! You will have your desires! Everyday is your birthday as you rise brand new each day, reborn to handle and face yourself, that is our only hurdle! Happy Birthday, may you begin to celebrate all you are and will become!

Electrons

Keep my mind free, loved ones please pray for me That I am able to see what's as elusive as a breeze It's ok my mind is a positive and able to attract That's why I focus on no lack I just give more and get that back Now that's a scientific fact as 1+1 is 2.

That what you do to others will surely be done unto you.

To state that much more plain we will be judged for actions and deeds.

It is not the sin that befalls the son, it's truly what he sees.

Because as we think so as we are again in the scientific realm.

Negative captain or positive captain it is you who's at the helm What you think you see please believe me that life is lived in the spiritual place.

That look of wonder was had in mind before it ever reached your face.

Electrons make atoms and molecules are next Which forms the mass of the things you amass with all the wasted checks.

But think of this if but for a blink or the time it takes a grin to fade What we could do if constructive and true all our thoughts were made!

Spring

Brand new, refreshed and ready for a another cycle! As I age, I truly see the magnificence in a plan; that I could not possibly be meant to understand! So I just praise it, for the beauty it holds and the feelings that are inspired! The righteous hand of God that is found in nature. That thing, that supports our very life! Unable to be taken for granted when upset, you die; to be reborn every spring! Colors, bright; changing to a beat of an unheard drum. An orchestra seen but not heard, but the symphony is real. As the surrounding life joins in to add the score. Crickets playing the xylophone, as the birds sing alto. Spring, your beauty is GOD! As we all await your return and lament your passing! Joyful we are, for you!

Anything

Anything I would do to help you understand these laws that are showing me, what true power really is. We focus, so much on the synthetic rules of man to channel our forces through. When real power, lies in the manual it was copied from. The law of Attraction, the law of retaliation, the law of compensation, the law of cause and effect are but to name a few. These laws of the universe are immutable, they always work. The cosmos would be chaos, if not built on this ABSOLUTE TRUTH. Your thoughts are things. We daily are writing the story of our lives, with every notion we have. Every thought that lingers, brings forth its physical counterpart. This is evidence, of your power; to create. Watch what you wish for, NO plan on what you contemplate! Let it be for mankind's betterment and you will accomplish the amazing. We think of the trivial, not lofty aspirations. A man can only rise as high as his highest thought! So much power bestowed on us must be governed, or it will destroy; you and all you frequent! Read and discover, the blueprint of yourself. We are capable of so much, the law of the master mind will amaze you. Anything I would do! Jesus gave his life for us to discover that, "Whoever believes in me will do the works that I have been doing, and they will do even better things than these." If that is the TRUTH, which immutable it is so must be. In belief, we are able to do ... ANYTHING!

This fish bowl

We live in our neighborhoods, our jobs. We all assimilate, blend in. In this attempt we lose ourselves. In this tank no longer are we original, no longer are we ourselves. Yes, you are you but with a bit of this and a bit of that. So many extra pieces, that we no longer resemble the original. Let us retain the us, inside! What's so wrong with you, that you must change? Change if you must, but keep the you; you are perfect. Grow you will but don't lose you. That part you think isn't good enough, or won't be liked! That is the real you, develop that one. Don't be like the others. But be the new, incredible species that you are! Original, and absolutely perfect; in every way!

Try

Try to live loving yourself instead, of the opposite! So little effort is given to we! Our focuses, are everything but! Let's try to care for ourselves with the compassion we do our children, our loved ones and our friendships! Always there for each, but a slow arrival, if not a no show; for us! Every ounce of neglect, is an early shovel full of dirt that we heap on our graves! Buried alive, in the name of service! Can we try, for the sake of this one life we've been given? Or will we follow our nobility, to a premature burial? Loving others, more than ourselves! Let's TRY, to do better; by us. You can only love others, as much as you love yourself!

Just a matter of time

It's just a matter of time before we all understand. How long, can we needlessly suffer? It doesn't matter if a few understand, if one suffers; so do we all. The light is so close, just step through. It's just a matter of time, darkness is so lonely! The light has been inviting you home, all of your life. Peace, be still! It's just a matter of time, before the piece of God spills out of us; all and reassembles! Until we realize that love is just that. Until we know that as we do for others, we really pamper ourselves. Indeed, until we love simply for the sake of loving—and nothing else. Before no motives, lead our intent! Before this, is our way of life! It's just a matter of time, before we are free!

I order my steps

Outlandish statements, blaspheming, misleading and untrue! Think as thow will. I order my steps with the ease of my character, because it is my guide! As I think, I am. So righteous I will be. Not always, but enough to forever change myself; so that perfection is my new normal! Given credit for every attempt, so as we try we inch closer and closer; triumphing even in failure. What we think about we receive. I order my steps, because I refuse to think any thing other than success, courage, strength and helpfulness! I live to serve and serve to live. I plan courageously and execute fearlessly! Yes, I order my steps, like the foot prints in the sand.